D1259535

LITTLE MIX

SHOUT OUT TO BRITAIN'S GREATEST GIRL GROUP

Malcolm Mackenzie

CONTENTS

THE BEST GIRLBAND

IN THE WORLD

Over the years Little Mix have become a British institution, like the royal family, Harry Potter and builder's tea! Frankly, they deserve an award. Oh wait – they've got loads.

Little Mix have done something that girlbands almost never do: they stayed together. And because of that simple fact they have continued to entertain and delight fans year after year, going from strength to strength. Since Little Mix were put together on *The X Factor* in 2011 they have had four number one singles, five top five albums and their songs have been streamed an incredible eleven billion times.

They may have found fame in the UK on a British TV show, but they have had success all over the world, from Europe to Australia, Asia to America.

The power of the girls lies in their incredibly catchy and consistently excellent music and in their super-likeable personalities. Unlike some pop stars, Little Mix remain down to earth and totally relatable despite their success and wealth.

Never known to shy away from a cause, Little Mix stand up and say what's on

their minds. They have addressed online bullies and body shamers, they have spoken up about their personal struggles with mental health issues, and leant their voice to open the conversation about misogyny, race, sexuality and identity.

These girls are brave and they take chances – whether it's stripping off for a video, coming back with a totally unexpected new sound, wearing far-out fashions or simply saying what no other pop star would dream of – Little Mix kill it.

The one thing that fans of Little Mix love as much as the bops, the videos and the brilliant live shows is the fact that the four girls are best friends. They genuinely love and support each other. They've stuck together through all the ups and downs and unlike many girlbands there are almost never reports of feuds, jealousy or infighting – and that's the true definition of girl power.

LM THROUGH THE YEARS

2011

SHOUT OUT TO THE X FACTOR

Simon Cowell may be TV's big meanie, but we will always love him for giving us Little Mix.

MAKING MAGIC

Little Mix were not born, they were created. All four girls auditioned as solo singers for the eighth series of *The X Factor* in 2011 but failed to make it past the bootcamp stage. They were then put in groups Faux Pas and Orion, before finally being brought together for the four-piece, Rhythmix.

SAME NAME

At first the group were called Rhythmix, but because a children's music charity already had that name they changed it to the catchy and cute Little Mix, which is simpler and much more fun.

> Series eight, which gave us LM, had the third highest ratings of any X Factor.

SUPER ACE

The very first song Little Mix performed was Nicki Minaj's *Superbass*. Gary Barlow loved it, instantly declaring them "the best girlband that has ever been on *The X Factor*". Apologies to Belle Amie, Bad Lashes and The Conway Sisters.

The girls urge viewers to vote while they grab a few essentials.

Little Mix make their TV debut.

Perrie showcases her powerful vocals.

BIG HITTER

CANNONBALL

For the winners' single, Little Mix released a cover of Damien Rice's ballad *Cannonball*. It would become the fastest selling single of 2011, shifting 210,000 copies in a week, and outselling the rest of the top five combined.

SLOW START

For the first month Janet Devlin was the audience favourite, but on week seven Little Mix captured the nation's hearts and ears with a rendition of *Don't Let Go (Love)* by 90s American girl group En Vogue.

HAIR MARE

Both Jesy and Leigh-Anne have said that *The X Factor* stylists ruined their hair. Thankfully it is looking great now!

Little Mix were the first ever group to win *The X Factor*. JLS came second and One Direction only came third – can you believe it?

The newly formed foursome hit the red carpet.

IT'S IN THEIR DNA

8 REASONS
LITTLE MIX ROCK!

We can think of four pretty obvious reasons to love Little Mix, here are eight more.

1 They have the most incredible voices

Some groups have members who are there for their looks or their personality but not Little Mix, everyone is also a bona fide vocal cracker!

2 They are comedy legends

Never has a girl group been this funny. All the girls have a wicked sense of humour and are just as likely to make us laugh as they are sing along. They don't take themselves too seriously: they leave that to the fans – screeeam!!!

3 They're incredibly down to earth

Most girlbands are down to earth and relatable at the start of their careers, but then they become mega stars and gain an attitude to match. Not LM, they are just as 'real' as they ever were.

4 Girls can perform

When so much pop music is standing around singing, it's refreshing to see an act like Little Mix – they can kill a dance routine, sing flawlessly and really get a crowd going.

5 Their songs are all-time classics

When *Black Magic*, *Touch* or *Shout Out To My Ex* comes on the radio everything stops. Whoever you are – mums, nans, dads – you can't help singing and fist-pumping along.

6 They really do MIX it up

You never know what Little Mix will do next. They constantly keep us guessing, working with cool producers (eg: Cheat Codes), collaborating with exciting artists (eg: Stormzy) and changing their sound (eg: Reggaeton) and look, at the drop of a floppy wide-brimmed hat.

7 The fashions

What other group causes frontpage headlines every time they step out the house in a new outfit? Whether they're dressing down or are dolled up to the nines, their mix – that word again – of designer and high street, girly and boyish, scruffy and smart is irresistible.

8 They actually like each other

Every girlband in the history of forever split up because they couldn't get along or one of them wanted to hog the spotlight. Watching LM live or in interviews it's clear that they have a lot of love for each other, and no single person ever dominates: sharing is caring, people.

JESY NELSON

Full name: Jessica Louise Nelson
Date of birth: 14 June 1991
Hometown: Romford, Essex

12 THINGS YOU NEED TO KNOW ABOUT

JESY

Listen up! Here are some important information nuggets about Jesy Nelson.

1
Jesy was an extra in *Harry Potter and The Goblet of Fire*. She was in the ballroom scene: jels.

2
Before *The X Factor*, Jesy worked in a bar. Her mum told her to get a better job – so she did.

3
Her worst habit is taking ages to get ready.

4
Jesy says if she wasn't famous she'd love to go to a festival and get stuck in with the crowd.

5
Jesy's first album was the Spice Girls.

6
Jesy collects trainers and has hundreds of pairs all boxed up.

7
When Jesy was about 13 her hair started falling out – a stress condition called alopecia.

8
Jesy wanted to be a professional sprinter – she was the fastest 100 metre runner in her borough.

9
Her mum used to do her washing for her – even after she left home.

10
She loves a cockney boy – and has a crush on Danny Dyer.

11
She has a sweet tooth and loves party rings biscuits, Haribo and Easter eggs.

12
She has a history of going commando – not wearing any pants.

2012

TAKING FLIGHT

Little Mix join a select club of stars that leave *The X Factor* and achieve massive global success.

FOUR TO THE TOUR

From February to April 2012, Little Mix toured the UK with fellow favourites from *The X Factor* – Misha B, Amelia Lily, The Risk and who can forget Kitty Brucknell? The girls performed six songs including popular numbers from the TV show like *E.T.* by Katy Perry and *Don't Let Go (Love)*.

WINGS

The first proper Little Mix single *Wings* went straight to number one, going platinum with sales of 716,000. The anthem about brushing off bullies and believing in yourself went to number three in Australia, number seven in Japan and even charted in America, making the girls an international force to be reckoned with.

DNA DAY

Both the *DNA* single, and album of the same name, reached number three in the UK charts, and the album went straight in at number four in the US, beating even the Spice Girls whose first album *Spice* debuted at number six. Girl power indeed.

Was there a greater *X Factor* tour?

FLYING OFF SHELVES

2012 really was the year of Little Mix merch. The fandom was growing and the appetite for everything Leigh-Anne, Perrie, Jesy and Jade was massive, so thankfully they released their first official book, *Ready To Fly*, to help us get to know the girls a bit better and the fact it was packed with gorgeous pictures didn't hurt.

FEAR FACTOR

When the girls performed their dramatic single *DNA* on the ninth series of *The X Factor* it was like coming home, but Perrie said that whenever they return to the show it's really stressful and makes her feel a bit sick, because they have to prove why they won. She needn't worry. The girls' vocals are always totally on point.

MOVE OVER BARBIE

Any self-respecting pop band needs a collection of dolls, but capturing a likeness proved to be a bit a challenge for manufacturers of the Little Mix toys. Leigh-Anne and Perrie did alright, but despite their magnificent hair Jesy and Jade were unrecognisable.

Young mixers ran to Primark to buy an exclusive range of clothes for 7-13 year olds.

2012 was a year of firsts for Little Mix: they went to their first BRIT Awards, Party in The Park and the Jingle Bell Ball.

Little Mix were a colourful addition to the pop landscape.

LITTLE MIX IN
NUMBERS

Wanna know why Little Mix are so amazing? Let's figure it out.

50 million
The amount of records singles and albums Little Mix are estimated to have sold.

28/10/2011
The date Little Mix were created.

3
The number of times Jade auditioned for *The X Factor* before being put in Little Mix.

12+ million
The number of followers Little Mix have on Instagram.

23
The number of songs Little Mix have had in the UK top 40.

63
The number of countries *Glory Days* went top 10 on iTunes.

4
The amount of number one UK singles.

3 billion
The number of YouTube views they've had.

30
The number of years between Little Mix's *Bounce Back* and *Back to Life*, the song that inspired it by Soul II Soul.

£6.6 million
The amount Little Mix earned between Aug 2017 and Aug 2018.

582 million

The number of views *Black Magic* has had on YouTube. It's their most viewed song.

0

The number of tattoos Perrie has. Jesy has over 10.

12+ million

Number of subscribers Little Mix have on YouTube.

6

The number of times Little Mix have been nominated for the Pop Justice £20 Music Prize.

LM ARE
STYLE QUEENS

When Little Mix stride out onto the red carpet, prepare to be stunned, wowed and inspired.

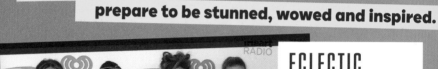

ECLECTIC GLAMOUR

You could argue that Little Mix don't look like a girlband here, but four stylish indi-visuals. Sometimes they want to assert their personalities and that's fantastic.

THEY WEAR THE TROUSERS

There's nothing more chic than a pair of wide-leg or tapered trousers: they mean business, and keep you warm to boot – boots optional, obviously.

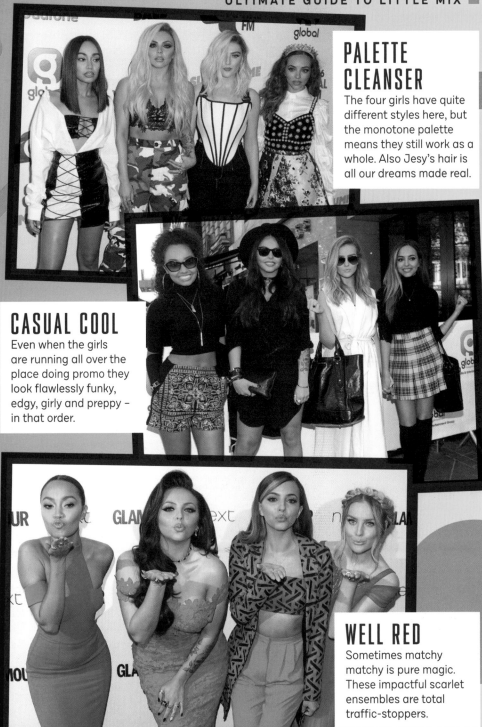

PALETTE CLEANSER

The four girls have quite different styles here, but the monotone palette means they still work as a whole. Also Jesy's hair is all our dreams made real.

CASUAL COOL

Even when the girls are running all over the place doing promo they look flawlessly funky, edgy, girly and preppy – in that order.

WELL RED

Sometimes matchy matchy is pure magic. These impactful scarlet ensembles are total traffic-stoppers.

2013

A MOVE IN THE RIGHT DIRECTION

The girls prove they're no fluke with a cracking second album and an edgy new sound – ooh so sharp, ouch!

HOW YA DOIN'?

When Little Mix released *How Ya Doin'?* it was a star-studded affair. Not only was the song co-written by All Saints' Shaznay Lewis it featured rap legend Missy Elliot. To promote the single they hired an ice cream van for the day and gave out free ice cream – because who doesn't love Mr Whippy?

ATTEN-SHUN!

The girls co-wrote 12 of the 16 songs on their harder, military-influenced second album *Salute* and according to Perrie they recorded all the vocals for the album in just 12 days. Leigh-Anne described the intense process as 'gruelling,' but it was well worth it – the album got to number four in the UK and number six in the US.

HEADLINE HERE

For their first headline tour, Little Mix took a quick whizz around the UK and Ireland and were finished within a month. As well as playing songs from their debut album, they sang a couple of covers – but not their first number one hit, *Cannonball* – which the girls weren't massive fans of in the first place.

How WE doin? Much better now we have free ice cream, ta.

MOVING ON

When Little Mix released sparse R&B comeback song *Move* people weren't sure if the girls had made a big mistake, but then they listened again, saw the amazing video and fell in love. Phew – even the girls agreed that they'd taken a risk, with Jade admitting, "It's so quirky and different – I'd definitely say we've gone a bit cooler with this one." She wasn't even a little bit wrong.

YOU BEAUTY!

In 2013 the girls helped fans look cool by collaborating on a series of hair and beauty products, including Schwarzkopf LIVE Colour XXL, Elegant Touch press-on nails and nail wraps and a make-up collection, for, erm, Collection.

EXPORT FACTOR

Thanks to their stateside success the girls appeared at massive showbiz events like the Nickelodeon Kids' Choice Awards (pictured below) and even scooped the Ultimate Export award at the 2013 Cosmo Awards.

Jesy admitted that Ian Beale is her guilty pleasure.

Little Mix escape being slimed at the Kids' Choice Awards.

Perrie got engaged to Zayn Malik. You can spot the whopper diamond ring he gave her in the video to *Love Me Like You*.

21

WORD UP!

7 secrets behind Little Mix songs and the craft of creating some of our favourite tunes of all time.

Winging it

Wings may be one of the oldest Little Mix songs but it still holds a remarkable power for Leigh-Anne. She admits that whenever she hears the song or performs it live, she still believes 100% of every single word she sings about standing up to bullies: "The message is so strong, that it can make you feel so much better about everything," she confesses.

2 DNA: Delusional Nutso Affection?

Around the time of release, Perrie described *DNA* as a love song, but Leigh-Anne went further to suggest that it's about a love verging on obsession. She even used the example of Facebook stalking – not a great idea – but this reading of the song certainly offers a dark twist to match the intensity of the vocal delivery.

3 Womenspiration

Perrie believes that the girls write songs about whatever comes into their heads, but does admit that more often than not, it tends to be a girl power anthem.

4 All hail Salute

After the girls finished recording mega bop *Salute*, they begged the record company to give them a rough copy because they loved it so much and couldn't wait for the final fully-produced version. As soon as they got it Perrie says they blasted it over and over and over, because Little Mix are in fact Mixers.

5 Won't work

Little Mix have described *I Won't*, the song they wrote with Jess Glynne, as their most personal. The powerful anthem (of course) came out of the frustration of having writer's block and not knowing what to write next. When the girls were feeling particularly down and defeated Jess gave the girls an encouraging pep talk and what do you know? They wrote *I Won't*, a happy-clappy tune packed with good vibes and positive affirmations.

6 Strip advisor!

Jesy describes the song *Strip* as a 'turning point' for the girls, who've stood against the full scrutiny of the media

not to mention the cruelty of social media for many years. She went on to say that, despite suffering from body confidence issues and bullying in the past, that now the girls are over it, and feel good about themselves and they can finally address the issue in *Strip*: "That one song where we've really said it how it is."

7 Jade spits Wasabi

The fan favourite from *LM5*, which serves classic *Blackout* Britney, came from a real-life situation where one of Little Mix's collaborators was eating sushi laden with ultra-spicy wasabi. Jade was so stunned by the amount of mouth-burning wasbi being consumed she said, "How are you eating that? If it was me, I would just spit it out." And suddenly the idea for a hot song was born.

LEIGH-ANNE PINNOCK

Full name: Leigh-Anne Pinnock

Date of birth: 4 October 1991

Hometown: High Wycombe, Buckinghamshire

12 THINGS YOU NEED TO KNOW ABOUT

LEIGH-ANNE

Bet you don't know all these snippety bits of intel about Leigh-Anne Pinnock.

1
Leigh-Anne was head girl and the captain of the basketball team at school – get her.

2
Rihanna once told Leigh-Anne that her hair was awesome.

3
Leigh-Anne went vegan in 2018.

4
Before Little Mix, Leigh-Anne worked at Pizza Hut and would nick the dough.

5
Her very weird celeb crush is Jeremy Kyle.

6
Nothing stops Leigh-Anne from going out and partying.

7
She loves dogs so much she was even made an ambassador of Battersea dogs home. Bow WOW!

8
She used to get teased for having acne.

9
When Leigh-Anne passed her driving test she vowed never to get on a bus again.

10
Leigh-Anne was rushed to A&E when she burnt her leg making hot Vicks.

11
She once threw up and passed out in HMV.

12
Leigh-Anne enjoys cleaning, especially the bathroom.

LM
THROUGH
THE
YEARS

2014

SALUTE TO SUCCESS

Little Mix embark on their first proper arena tour, and release a funky single for Sport Relief.

EXERCISE GUYS

Because Little Mix's cover version of Cameo's *Word Up* was for the Sport Relief charity, the energetic music video saw the girls pulling their gym gear on and taking a spin, lifting some weights and turning full-on teacher to hold a massive aerobics class. Think how much easier it would be to motivate yourself to go to the gym if Little Mix really did hold keep fit classes.

4 BECOME 6

Like *Word Up*, *Salute* got to number six in the UK singles chart. The single came out in April 2014 and was their last release for the year, which was one of the quietest for the group, who were beavering away in the studio. They promoted the song with performances on *Britain's Got Talent* and jetted off to America to perform the song on American TV.

OH BOY

Perrie admitted that she would have quite liked to have released the album track *Boy* as another single from *Salute*. Despite being acapella – with no instruments – she thought that if radio had played the song people might have fallen in love with it anyway because the harmonies are that good.

The *Word Up* video is a bit of a stretch.

Girls on tour, on jeeps.

ARENAS ARE GO!

Little Mix went on their biggest tour yet and due to demand had to add dates and move to bigger venues to accommodate all the excitable Mixers. It took place from May to July and saw massive sets of scaffolding, props – hello massive jeep – and costume changes-a-plenty. As well as their own songs, Little Mix sang Katy Perry's *Dark Horse* and *Talk Dirty* by Jason Derulo.

ACCENT CHALLENGE

As fans of *Downton Abbey*, Americans can get quite the shock when they hear real British accents, as Jade discovered when she travelled to the US. She admitted that she tries to tone down her Newcastle accent to help them understand her better. Hilariously some yanks think Jade's name is Jeed, because of the way she pronounces it – say it out loud: Jeed – Lol.

HOORAY FOR TODAY

In June, when Little Mix appeared on *The Today Show* in America it was a big deal, not least because the programme, which gets a massive audience, showcased the girls' incredible talents with three performances. The girls sang *Wings*, *Little Me* and *Salute*.

Little Mix had to cancel the American leg of their *Salute* tour to finish working on the album that would become *Get Weird*, which was sad for fans, but worth it for the incredible 2015 comeback.

Little Mix perform on *The Today Show*.

27

LITTLE TIPS:
BEAUTY

If you love the way the girls look, take a leaf out of their beauty book.

JADE hates to leave the house without a brow pencil and a bit of lippy. She also loves a dab of highlighter.

When putting on blusher PERRIE thinks it's important to start with a tiny amount and build it up, because once it's on it's hard to take off.

JESY take ages to get ready doing her make-up first, then her hair. Because she's got really curly hair it takes a while to blow dry.

PERRIE rocks a strong brow, and loves it – don't over tweeze!

LEIGH-ANNE is a massive fan of Australian skincare brand Aesop and uses the cleanser, toner and moisturiser. She says it helped to sort out her spot-prone skin.

LEIGH-ANNE's two make-up essentials are powder and lipstick.

PERRIE and JADE always carry eyelash glue, because their falsies never stay put on a night out. They're also addicted to dry shampoo because they both hate washing their hair.

LEIGH-ANNE has a trés sophisticated nose and wears perfumes from Lancome, Chanel and Victor and Rolf while JADE prefers good old Britney Spears – Curious.

Can't get the perfect winged eyeliner? Try gel liner – JADE is a massive fan and says it's easier to apply than liquid eyeliner.

Red lipstick gives JESY an instant pick-me-up while PERRIE loves daring lip colours like purple.

JESY and LEIGH-ANNE both swear by argan oil for shiny manageable hair. PERRIE suggests putting a hair mask on under a showercap for an even more intense treatment and sleeping with it on overnight.

JESY gets make-up inspiration from beauty influencers on Instagram – she screenshots her faves.

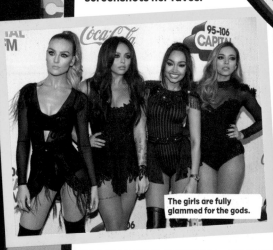

The girls are fully glammed for the gods.

LITTLE MIX'S NOT SO...
SECRET LOVES

Because everyone needs a little bit of loving and a hugging, especially after a world tour!

LEIGH-ANNE SCORES BIG

2016 was a good year for finding love for the Mixers. Leigh-Anne met her Watford footballer boyf Andre Gray and despite their hectic schedules they have been inseparable ever since. After two years together Leigh-Anne posted a loved-up message saying she wanted to spend the rest of her life with him, *reaches for tissue*.

ROCK WITH YOU

Jade dated Jed Elliot, bassist with the rock band The Struts, from 2016 to 2019 and they made the cutest couple. She had to chase him and even tried to be a bit of a rock chick to catch his eye – but in the end she realised that being yourself is always the best option. Damn, they were a fine-looking pair.

PERRIE LIVER-PULLS

Perrie sure can pick them. For a while she was dating one of the biggest pop stars in the world, Zayn Malik, but since 2016 she's been seeing Alex Oxlade-Chamberlain, one of the best footballers in the country. In 2017 he signed a five-year deal for Liverpool worth £35 million – think of the Milky Bars (her fave) he could buy Pezza with that?

For four glorious years, Perrie and Zayn were pop's super couple and even got engaged. Some of us still aren't over the split.

NO RUSH FOR LOVE

Like Perrie and Zayn, we thought Jesy had met 'the one' when she fell for and got engaged to Jake Roche from the band Rixton, but it wasn't to be. We thought she was great with Diversity's Jordan Banjo and musician Harry James, but some relationships aren't meant to last, so you chalk it up to experience and move on.

Recently, Jesy has been dating Chris Hughes from TV's *Love Island*. Chris was shown supporting Jesy in her documentary about online bullying *Odd One Out*.

LM THROUGH THE YEARS

2015

STILL MAKING MAGIC

Little Mix must *really* have taken a sip from a secret potion because everyone fell in love with them.

Little Mix launch their first fragrance.

BLACK MAGIC

No one was prepared for the phenomenon that was *Black Magic*. When the girls came back with this massive single and brilliant accompanying video, the world went bananas. It went straight to number one in the UK chart and stayed there for three weeks and became their biggest hit in the US. It also charted in Australia, Japan, Mexico and Canada, not to mention all over Europe. Unsurprisingly it was nominated for best single and video at the 2016 BRIT Awards.

EAU DE GIRLBAND

Released in time for summer, Little Mix launched their very first secret potion/perfume: *Gold Magic*. The delicious scent has fruity notes, a powdery violet heart and deep musky warmth. The girls wanted to make sure younger fans enjoyed the fragrance, but it was still sophisticated enough that older Mixers fell under its spell too.

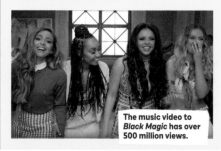

The music video to *Black Magic* has over 500 million views.

WONDERFULLY WEIRD

As album titles go, 2015's *Get Weird* seems like a bit of an odd one, but as Perrie explained at the time: "We are weird, and we based the album on that." There's no arguing with such solid logic. We are ALL a bit weird. The girls' third album was about embracing who you are including all the nutty peculiar bits, because those are the most special.

LOVE SICK

The second single from *Get Weird, Love Me Like You*, was their least weird song ever: the midtempo singalong was a classic-sounding throwback to girlbands from the 60s. The video set in a school dance featured all the girls pining after a boy at a school dance – a timeless theme for a timeless song.

PRETTY GOOD WRITERS

Little Mix are not just amazing singers and performers they also write a mean tune, which is why Britney Spears and Iggy Azalea snapped up the song co-written by LM: *Pretty Girls*. The song reached number 16 in the UK and Britney regularly performed it in Vegas.

THE GIFT OF SWIFT

The collab of the century happened when Taylor Swift brought the girls on stage with her in Santa Clara, California during her *1989* Tour. The fab fivesome performed *Black Magic* and it was a joy to behold. Little Mix confessed it was one of the best experiences of their Little Mix lives. Wildest dreams do come true.

Much to the sadness of One Direction and Little Mix fans, Perrie and Zayn confirmed that they had split up in August 2015. Perrie later revealed that she found out they were no longer an item by text. Way harsh, Zayn.

The girls take the *Black Magic* video 'geeks' to the Teen Choice Awards.

IN THEIR OWN WORDS

Out of the mouths of total babes. Little Mix are real, honest and utterly hilarious!

RUNNING SCARED

"I did the 400 metres (at school) but I hadn't trained so I came last. As I got to the end I was nearly sick."
- LEIGH-ANNE

SPIN CYCLE

"Me first kiss happened with a boy from school in Year 6, when I was 11. I didn't know what I was doing – it was a bit of a washing machine situation."
- JADE

PYJAMARAMA

"I go to the shops in my PJs all the time! Especially when I'm with my best friend Catherine – we'll have cravings for crisps and snacks, so we'll drive to the 24-hour Tesco." *- PERRIE*

DELIVER-BOOOO

"I do feel very sorry for the boy who marries me, because they're not going to get any dinner. Just Deliveroo every night." *- JESY*

PARP STARS

"We always share a bed (on tour). So we're all in bed together and we've all got wind. And we thought it would be funny to put it on Instagram. Farting on cue." – *LEIGH-ANNE*

GRAN DESIGNS

"Somebody tweeted and said his grandma could sing better than us. I tweeted back and said, 'Bring your Nana over and we'll have a listen'. I wish he did!" **– JADE**

WOTSIT MEAN?

"I love Chicken & Mushroom Pot Noodle with Wotsits. It's so good! You don't have to mix the Wotsits in, you just sprinkle them on top like croutons!" **– PERRIE**

HAT'S ENOUGH

"Leigh-Anne's the naughtiest. When we were on the *X Factor* tour she got Derry's (from boyband The Risk) hat and poured drink and crisps in it. He was really upset – not crying, but annoyed." **– JESY**

BEE CALM

"I was sitting on this swing and had this bee sit on my nose for an hour. As soon I moved, it stung me." **– JADE**

FLASH AHHHHH

"This is going to sound weird but I love the smell of Flash. I actually enjoy cleaning, especially the bathroom." **– LEIGH-ANNE**

MIXER MADNESS

"American fans definitely scream loads. You can say anything. You could say 'poo' and they'd cry." **– JESY**

BAD BREATH

"Sometimes I'd do interviews and people would be like, what's that noise and it would be me breathing in the corner." **– PERRIE** *(before she had her tonsils removed)*

Little Mix are the number *choice* for pop star LOLs

PERRIE EDWARDS

Full name: Perrie Louise Edwards
Date of birth: 10 July 1993
Hometown: South Shields, Tyne & Wear

12 THINGS YOU NEED TO KNOW ABOUT

PERRIE

Absolutely essential information you need to know about Perrie Edwards.

1
Perrie's mum and dad are both singers too.

2
If she could be any Disney Princess it would be Sleeping Beauty, because she loves a good nap.

3
Perrie does an amazing impression of a goat.

4
Her first kiss was on the beach looking at the stars when she was 17. Romantic much?

5
She doesn't have a sense of smell.

6
She's dated two of the world's cutest men: Zayn Malik and Luke Pasqualino.

7
When Perrie got her first Little Mix pay check she bought furniture for her flat.

8
Jake Gyllenhaal is her celebrity crush.

9
Perrie moved to New Zealand for a year and a half when she was 10 years old.

10
Chocolate is her weakness – she loves Milky Bar.

11
Growing up Perrie wanted to be a vet.

12
She runs like a headless chicken – her words not ours.

LM THROUGH THE YEARS

2016

GIRLBAND GLORY DAYS

In 2015 Little Mix were on fire, in 2016 they followed their amazing success with more of the flaming same.

TIME TO GO PRO

After getting a taste for fitness doing Sport Relief, the girls became brand ambassadors for athleisure brand USA Pro. The girls were super-excited to help design their own range of gym gear to fit all body shapes and sizes. The clothes, which included leggings, vests, sports bras and trainers, looked so good, it was just as wearable down the shops as it was in aerobics.

EX-STATIC

Little Mix enjoy their biggest ever hit with *Shout Out To My Ex*, a tongue-in-cheek break-up anthem that Taylor Swift would be proud of. The girls debuted the single on their spiritual home, *The X Factor*, and it went to number one for three weeks. The video, which sees the girls tearing through a Spanish desert in a convertible, has over 300 million views on Vevo alone.

GLORY, HALLELUJAH

When *Glory Days* stayed at number one for a whopping four weeks, it equalled the record for most weeks at number one by a girlband this millennium, matching Destiny's Child's *Survivor* in 2001. They have a long way to go to beat the record of 15 weeks at no.1 by the Spice Girls with *Spice*.

Behind the scenes filming on the USAPro advert.

HARD WORK PAYS OFF

Little Mix were enjoying so much success in 2016 that the year marked the first time the girls made more than £1 million each in a single year. The cash injection came courtesy of their massive singles and sell out tours, not to mention merchandise deals.

A TOUCHING TUNE

Finger-clicking tropical banger *Touch* was an unseasonable December release to evoke the ideal summer holiday not Christmas by a log fire. It only got to number four in the chart, but fans couldn't get enough and it hung around for yonks raking up plays, streams and downloads galore till it became their third biggest single ever.

A WORLD OF SHOCKS

When Little Mix released their book, *Our World*, Mixers were surprised by how candid and open the girls were. Perrie described her break-up with Zayn as the worst time of her life, Jade spoke about her battle with eating disorders, and Jesy opened up about her experiences with bullying.

Little Mix were getting so big that winning awards started to become common place. In 2016 they picked up the MTV Europe Award for best UK and Ireland act, Teen Choice Award for International Artist and Glamour Award for Music Act of the Year: bish, bash, bosh.

LM SURE CAN
MOVE!

Little Mix make music that's excellent to dance to, so it's a good job that they can swivel a hip.

Choo choo choo
All board the Little Mix train to Funky Town – first stop, Sparkleville.

Lean green machine
Perrie tackles the tricky 'switch the light off and flush the loo with your foot' manoeuvre.

Feeling cross
Leigh-Anne wants you to stop! In the name of mesh.

Hop to it

If you've ever tried yoga you'll know that this variant of 'tree pose' is particularly difficult. Ommm-g!

Cuts a dash

Jesy is either about to do that weird skeleton arms thing, or quickly run off stage for a scrunchie.

Big birds

When someone tells you to 'shake your tailfeather,' they're usually just being cute, but Little Mix actually do shake their tailfeathers ... and shoulder feathers and arm ribbons.

Little kick

If Little Mix did music boxes this is what you'd find twirling around feistily inside.

LITTLE TIPS:
STYLE

Fashion is supposed to be fun, so make like Little Mix, experiment and dress how you want.

Evolve

You don't have to stick with one look you know? Little Mix have evolved over the years as their tastes have changed and you can follow suit – although you don't have to wear a suit.

Never be afraid to experiment

Jesy reckons if you like something, you should wear it and if people don't like it, that's their problem. Be strong and whack the thing on.

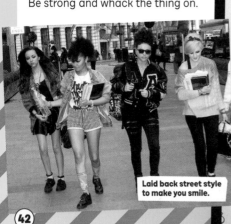

Laid back street style to make you smile.

Fully embrace the high street

When Little Mix first started and made some real money for the first time in their lives, they didn't rush to Harvey Nicks to stock up on Gucci and Chanel – Jesy splurged at All Saints and Perrie, keeping it realer than real, emptied the aisles of her local Primark.

Do 'YOU!'

The girls encourage you to dress for yourself, not for anyone else, be that your friendship group or a boy you fancy. Wear what you like and what makes *you* feel good, and before you know it, people will be looking to you for style advice.

Find something you love

Leigh-Anne absolutely adores bikinis and has even declared swimwear her favourite type of clothing. Lucky Leigh gets to go on holiday more than most of us, so maybe your signature garment will be wellies or a cardie.

Stan a star

Take a leaf out of Perrie's book and find a celebrity whose style you love, and let their inspiration be yours. Perrie has said that early Madonna and 90s TV shows like *Saved By The Bell* were a fashion inspiration to her.

Experiment with colour

The Little Mix girls love monochrome and subtle autumnal shades, but they also love a daring pop of colour. Don't be shy, give hot pink a try.

Learn what works

Like Little Mix, we all come in different shapes and sizes with a range of skin tones. Make a note of what colours suit you, what styles flatter and make you feel confident, then work more of those pieces into your wardrobe. It's what Little Mix have been doing for years.

LM THROUGH THE YEARS

2017

POWER UP

There were highs and lows, but 2017 cemented Little Mix as the biggest girl group in the world.

SHOUT OUT TO THE BRITS

Little Mix did it! They won best British single at The BRIT Awards. The looks of joy on their faces when they won was priceless. You never saw four happier women. It had been six long years since they won *The X Factor*, but they finally got the industry recognition they deserved when *Shout Out To My Ex* made their dreams come true.

COLLAB LAB

2017 was the year of collabs – Little Mix worked with Machine Gun Kelly on *No More Sad Songs*, CNCO on *Reggaeton Lento*, and most exciting of all, Stormzy on *The Power*. It's a testament to their incredible talent that the best artists in the world - Ariana, Taylor, Nicki Minaj and Missy Elliot – want to work with Little Mix. They really do have the power: grrrrrr.

This one's for Jake, Jordan, Sam and Zayn.

WISHMAKER PERFUME

As a fan of Little Mix, sight and sound are quite important, but so is scent, which is a shame for Perrie with her inability to smell. She presumably took a back seat when it came to the creation of Little Mix's second fragrance *Wishmaker*, a delicious vanilla apricot and neroli concoction.

Si-Co putting the CO in boyband CNCO.

SPANISH SENORITAS

Despacito was such a global smash for Justin Bieber that when Little Mix were asked to lend their magic touch to boyband CNCO's English remix of *Reggaetón Lento*, they sensibly jumped at the chance. The funky Latin dance number gave the girls yet another inescapable summer hit. Funnily enough the boys first found fame on a reality show called *La Banda* created by one Simon Cowell – small world huh?

77 DAYS OF GLORY

The older a band gets the better the tours become. By *The Glory Days* tour Little Mix had so many hit records that fans over the world were clamouring to see the girls and this time they went as far as Australia and Japan. The 77 show tour stretched from May 2017 to March 2018 – that's a lot of singing, dancing and rinsing tights in hotel bathrooms.

ONE LOVE MANCHESTER

Following the horrific bombing of Ariana Grande's *Dangerous Woman* tour in Manchester, Ariana threw a benefit concert for those directly affected by the tragedy. Little Mix leant their support performing an uplifting rendition of *Wings*. The girls joined Ari Justin Bieber, Katy Perry and Coldplay, to help raise a staggering £21 million.

Before Little Mix headed out on their own world tour they travelled America throughout February, March and April with Ariana Grande, opening the show on her *Dangerous Woman* tour.

Little Mix came together for One Love Manchester.

GIRLS ON TOUR

What happens on tour, stays on tour – unless the girls talked about it, then it's totes on these pages.

Little Mix have had six concert tours

2019: *LM5 Tour* (48 shows)

2018: *Summer Hits Tour* (15 shows)

2017: *Glory Days Tour* (77 shows)

2016: *Get Weird Tour* (60 shows)

2014: *Salute Tour* (20 shows)

2013: *DNA Tour* (23 shows)*

SLIP UP

One of the scariest moments ever to happen on tour took place during *The X Factor* tour way back in 2012. For one part of the show the girls had to fly over the stage hanging from the ceiling in harnesses, but for one performance while Jade was dancing in mid-air she tipped forward and nearly fell out of her harness. Oh My Gulp! The other girls didn't notice as poor Jade flipped about trying to turn herself back up the right way. Six months later Little Mix had wings – coincidence?

EDGE OF GLORY

The *Glory Days* tour is the girls' biggest ever tour and ranks as the fifth highest grossing concert tour by a girlband ever. It was seen by over 800,000 fans and grossed approximately 35 million pounds.

ANY REQUESTS

Before the girls played the 2015 *Jingle Bell Ball*, they had a couple of strange requests: Perrie asked for a puppy – actually not strange, a Spaniel would be heaven – while Jade put in an order for a medium rare steak with chip pan chips. They were only messing around, but it gives a rare insight into what a girlband really, really wants.

RITUAL HUGS

During the *Salute* tour Little Mix came up with a ritual they had to perform before every show: they would gather the dancers and the band and they would all put their hands into the middle of a circle and call out loud the words: "Attention hut! Attention hut! Attention hut! Attention salute!"

SUPPORTING SISTERS

As well as heading tours, Little Mix have also been the opening act for Ariana Grande and Demi Lovato. Despite not being the main event, the American fans go wild for the girls "They're very supportive. And a lot of the time, we see Little Mix T-shirts and Little Mix banners which makes us feel special," says Perrie.

TOO TOUR MUCH

Sometimes the hectic touring life can get a bit much. Leigh-Anne recently explained in an interview how the girls

ROUTINE BUSINESS

In 2014 Perrie described touring as: "The best time of our lives!" Why was she such a huge fan of being on the road? Well she loves performing, having the fans sing songs back to them, not to mention the lie-ins, "You're in a nice routine, it's nice to relax – literally touring is the best thing that could ever happen."

had all bought new houses but had never slept in them, while Jesy recalls getting home from a European tour and having to pack her bag to go off again, "I was looking at all of my suitcases and burst out crying. I was like: 'I can't do this.' Literally I nearly had a breakdown like, 'This is too much. I just want to be home.'"

JADE THIRLWALL

Full name: Jade Amelia Thirlwall

Date of birth: 26 December 1992

Hometown: South Shields, Tyne & Wear

12 THINGS YOU NEED TO KNOW ABOUT

JADE

Brace yourself for some extra diverting facts to surprise you, about Jade Thirlwall.

1
Jade was shortlisted to play Princess Jasmine at Disneyland Paris.

2
She has the worst eyesight in Little Mix and wears glasses for reading. She used to have a lazy eye.

3
Jade is fairly partial to a Toby Carvery.

4
When Jade travels she always takes tea bags, and a teddy to cuddle.

5
Jade hates clowns ever since she saw the film *IT*.

6
Jade has always loved to dance and used to win dance competitions as a kid in tap and ballet.

7
She has a tattoo that says 'anyone can achieve their dreams if they have courage'.

8
Due to a family joke, Jade used to think her mum was Diana Ross.

9
Jade loves putting things in boxes. Nice to have a hobby eh, Jade?

10
Her first album was by Craig David.

11
She used to have a pet beetle called Barry.

12
She is massive fan of *RuPaul's Drag Race* and Perrie says Jade's life ambition is to be a drag queen.

LM THROUGH THE YEARS

2018

WOMEN LIKE THEM RULE!

Little Mix came into their own – they were strong and outspoken, delivering powerful messages.

BIG CHEATS

American DJs Cheat Codes are some of the most in demand remixers out there having worked for Katy Perry, Steve Aoki and BTS, Niall Horan, Rita Ora, and Sam Smith. Their forays into original music produced *No Promises* with Demi Lovato which was great, but Little Mix's dreamy-bleepy *Love Island* anthem *Only You* was the absolute bomb.

SUMMER HITS TOUR

Presumably worn out after traipsing around the globe the previous year, Little Mix cooked up a little stay-at-home tour of the UK for 2018, playing smaller towns as a treat for Mixers who might not easily be able to travel to mega cities like London and Birmingham. The set list was a pure greatest hits selection of 16 songs, all killer, no filler, everyone a smash hit.

STRIP-EDY DOO DAH

When Little Mix were writing *LM5* they arrived at the studio having seen some nasty, judgemental things written about the way they look. Their co-writing colleague and friend Kamille started recording their conversation and when she played it back to them the empowering anthem of self-love *Strip* was born. The controversial video saw the girls naked covered in some of the cruel things that have been said to them over the years.

The brave ladies confront the trolls.

BEAUTY MADE SIMPLE

Little Mix have to wear make-up for their jobs, so you can bet they know a thing or two about it, which is why they released their first ever make-up range LMX at Boots. They also announced a collaboration with skincare brand Simple. Jade has been using their products since she was 12.

MTV Awards with Nicki Minaj – bosh!

LM5 COMES ALIVE

The fifth album by Little Mix didn't mess around, getting straight down to business delivering cracking tunes and the most experimental and grown-up record of their career so far, nailing every genre: trap, dub, tropical house, hip-hop, rock, rnb, and of course pop.

WINNING AT LIFE

The end of the year was massive for Little Mix, not only did they release their brilliant new album *LM5* they performed at the MTV Europe Awards with rap goddess Nicki Minaj and picked up the award for best group – UK and Ireland. They also snatched Best British Group at the Radio One Teen Awards. Pity the person that has to dust all the trophies.

Little Mix V5.0 are the sophisticated group we deserve.

Before Little Mix released *LM5* they parted ways with Simon Cowell's record imprint Syco, but they stuck with Sony, putting their fifth album out on the RCA label.

LITTLE MIX

GET WEIRD!

Little Mix are an attractive collection of sophisticated ladies. They're also a hilarious rabble of silliness.

Kiss and make-up
Little Mix: We prefer the natural make-up look. **Also Little Mix:** Rarrrrrrrrr!

Duckface selfie
A lot of celebrities want to look gorgeous in every photo, but not Leigh-Anne – she's totally quackers!

Flippin' 'eck
When you dance as much as Little Mix, you're liable to do your back in or crick your neck – but the real danger is trying not to lose your hair extensions.

Little Mystique

Jade might seem like the sweet cute one, but sometimes on Halloween she lets out her wild side and shows everyone that she's got the X-Men Factor.

Wigging out

Just because Little Mix are pop doesn't mean they can't rock, or at least do the finger thing and wear an itchy pink wig.

Quick Fit

The girls got fully behind the Sport Relief Campaign of 2014 releasing the single *Word Up*, flexing their muscles and pulling some serious gym faces – oooh yaaa!

LITTLE TIPS:
LIFE

Inspirational quotes from the queens who've been there, done it – bought the tiara.

"What we do to take care of ourselves when we're constantly on the grind is to have <u>GIRLY SLEEPOVERS</u> ... not wear any make-up, wear our onesies and eat loads of rubbish food, which isn't really taking care of ourselves, but it feels great." – *Jesy*

"Do not let anything hold you back – especially <u>THE COLOUR OF YOUR SKIN</u>, that's ridiculous. You literally have to go for it – put it into the universe, be positive and not let anything hold you back." – *Leigh-Anne*

"Social media can be so crap because it starts to mess with your head, and you start to feel like you're not good enough. It's about trying to differentiate what's real and what's not and a lot of the time, <u>SOCIAL MEDIA IS NOT REAL</u>." – *Perrie*

"I think everyone should be <u>HEARTBROKEN</u> at some point, to learn to be stronger." – *Jade*

"There's nothing wrong with <u>KISSING ON THE FIRST DATE!</u> I mean, it depends where the night takes you. It's not that bad." – *Jesy*

"If you've got loads going on in your head it can be impossible to shut off. <u>READING IN BED</u> helps me fall asleep straight away, so that makes me tired and I also listen to Stacey Kent's *Hushaby Mountain*. It's therapeutic." – *Perrie*

"We have a lot of LGBT fans and it's really important for us to encourage them to be who they are and to celebrate that through our music. It takes allies as well as the <u>LGBT COMMUNITY</u> to make a difference. Coming from a working-class town up north, where it is still very old-fashioned, I realise there's a long way to go." – *Jade*

Jade: marching for a better future.

"I used to be the shyest little thing ever. The thing that brought out my <u>CONFIDENCE</u> is being in this group with these girls. My tip is to surround yourself with positive people and good friends." – *Leigh-Anne*

LM THROUGH THE YEARS

2019

LITTLE MIX BOUNCE BACK

Things took a more serious turn in 2019, with each member opening up about their personal struggles.

HIGHEST CLIMBERS

Little Mix have always supported charitable causes, but when Leigh-Anne and Jade decided to climb the highest mountain in Africa for *Comic Relief*, fans were gobsmacked. The girls climbed 5895 metres to the summit of Kilimanjaro, suffering from altitude sickness, nausea, exhaustion and blisters. Jade described it as a life-changing experience, while Leigh-Anne said she realised that she was stronger than she could have imagined.

BOUNCY LADIES

Everyone loves a retro moment, so when Little Mix sampled *Back To Life* by Soul II Soul on their single *Bounce Back*, fans, and of course their mums and dads, approved. The video – one of their most colourful ever – imagines the girls as dolls in a world of never-ending pastels, leopard print and gold. Makes a change from Barbie pink.

LGBT TIME

Little Mix were honoured for their support of the LGBT+ community with a 'Change Makers' British LGBT Award. The award recognised the importance of LM featuring same-sex couples in the video to *Only You*, writing LGBT anthem *Secret Love Song*, marching at Manchester Pride, and Jade raising money for the Stonewall charity with her 25th birthday party.

Jade picks up an LGBT Award on behalf of Little Mix.

The BRIT Awards ate up the *Woman Like Me* video.

THE LM5 DRIVE

The end of the year saw the awesome foursome back on the road for their sixth tour to promote their album LM5. We hope that they've got a new tour bus, because in 2017 Perrie revealed that it wasn't exactly a state of the art affair, describing it as: "Cosy," but "quite old." Time for private jets, ladies?

BRIT OF ALRIGHT

If Little Mix thought their 2018 BRITs win was a fluke, they were in for a shock. The girls picked up yet another coveted award in 2019, this time for Best British Video, with *Woman Like Me*. The ultra-stylish clip was an absolute feast for the senses and a proper lol, showing the transformation of Perrie, Leigh-Anne, Jesy and Jade from perfect little ladies to wild wacky women, while Nicki Minaj channelled the paintings of Hogwarts – but sexier.

CONFESSION TIME

This year Little Mix opened up about the dark times in their lives. Jesy revealed that online bullies had pushed her to the very brink, Leigh-Anne discussed feeling invisible as the black member of the group, Perrie spoke about her crippling battle with anxiety, and Jade revealed that as a teenager her anorexia was life threatening. Their honesty was inspiring and started many much-needed conversations.

The best thing Little Mix created all year might've been *Eat In With Little Mix* – their YouTube *Come Dine With Me* inspired show. So funny. So quotable.

LITTLE MIX VS FAME

Sometimes being famous is amazing, sometimes it's the draggediest drag of all time.

COUNSELLING

After Little Mix released break-up anthem *Shout Out To My Ex* people started to treat Perrie like their personal agony aunt. Pezza revealed that strangers would come up to her in nightclubs and say that they felt so much better after hearing the hit song and that it changed their lives and made getting through their own relationship break ups that much easier.

CRAPARAZZI

Wherever the girls go you can bet there will be a man with a giant zoom lens snapping, which means the girls miss being able to do normal things without worrying about it being splashed on the front of tomorrow's newspaper. Jade says she misses, "Being able to look awful!" while Perrie doesn't enjoy trips to the seaside anymore: "Because as soon as they catch you bending over to fix your sand castle ... boom! picture!" So undignified.

24/7 STARDOM

Being in Little Mix isn't just a job that the girls can dip in and out of, they are always in the band, even on their days off. This inescapable truth is something Jesy is well aware of, and she explained it in the most hilarious Jesy-like fashion: "You can't un-famous yourself. You can't go 'Actually, I'm not working today', and pop to Tesco to fill up on snacks." She's not wrong y'know!

WISHMAKERS

If you think Little Mix have everything they could possibly want now they are mega-successful pop stars, think again. They still want a Nando's black card – a very rare thing given to celebrities that gets you as much free Nando's as you want. They also want to be immortalised in wax. Unbelievably Madame Tussauds have not crafted the girls in wax and they are getting tired of waiting.

NO MORE SAD ... EVER.

However Little Mix feel in their day to day lives, they try not to let it interfere with their schedule, which means that the girls have to do their best to seem happy all the time, which is crazy hard. Perrie likens the experience to being an actress while Leigh-Anne is lost for words trying to explain what it's like trying not to cry when that's all you want to do.

INSPIRATION

The stress of being in the public eye is worth it when the girls meet the fans. Sometimes it's young girls, sometimes it's the mums: Jesy recalls: "I was at the airport and this 40-year-old woman got out of her car. And she just started crying, and said: 'I came to your concert a week ago and you girls made me the most confident I've ever felt in my life. Can I give you a cuddle?'" #MRSMIXER

BATTLING ONLINE BULLIES

In her documentary with BBC Three, *Odd One Out*, Jesy revealed that online trolls were so relentless and vicious that she tried to end her life. Despite living her dream, the constant cruel taunts about her looks and weight actually made being in Little Mix a nightmare. Today Jesy avoids Twitter and says she's "a lot happier and mentally stronger."

DID YOUR FAVE MAKE IT?

LITTLE MIX

PARTY 20

Download this playlist to make any gathering of more than two people GO OFF!

1. *Black Magic*
The perfect pop song, that chugs along nicely enough, but when we hit the chorus it's total shout-along carnage.

2. *Shout Out To My Ex*
The most joyful reply to an ex-boyfriend. Jump up and down until your heel breaks, not your heart.

3. *Wings*
Little Mix are so darn good that their first proper single, *Wings*, is still a total thigh-slapping, foot stomping epic jam.

4. *Move*
A lowkey grower that grows so much it's already halfway to Mars. Clapping, humming, cheering and cowbells, you can't *not* move.

5. *Touch*
A sister song to Justin Bieber's *Sorry*, and just as genius. The tempo goes up and down till we explode – not literally.

6. *Power*
From the surf guitar to the squealing vocals, rat-tat drums, digi-squeals and bass whomp, there's no let up – so good.

7. *Private Show*
No it's not J-Lo or Pink, this is the greatest single that Little Mix never released. *Glory Days* was just too jam-packed.

8. *Woman Like Me*
From slinky mellow reggae to ballsy R&B, just try to stand still to this skittering track that was made for full-on twerking.

9. *Salute*
Ok ladies (and gents) now let's get in formation, it's time to jerk and snap your body to attention to the ultimate agro-pop.

10. *Reggaetón Lento*
Let your hips lead the way in this sultry number that speaks the universal language of catchy as hell.

11. *Wasabi*
Get ready to walk the runway with the spicy, staccato R&B pop track that's so cool you might need to grab your coat.

12. *No More Sad Songs*
Take an irresistible journey into tropical house, with a blissed-out club classic, that's far from sad.

13. *Hair*
The fantastic four get feisty in this clattering anthem about shaking off a boy that almost makes break-ups worth it.

14. *Only You*
Slow-building summer bop that starts so soothingly but builds from seductive toe-tapping to euphoric body-slamming.

15. *DNA*
Throwback Thursday to the dramatic, electric whoosh of LM's classic total 8-bit banger – altogether now D-D-D-DNA.

16. *Competition*
A jaunty shoulder-popping pop track with a solid 90s vibe and driving beat that you want to march/fling your arms around to.

17. *Change Your Life*
Put your arms in the air for the twinkly magic of this uplifting song then bring them together for the handclaps and head sway.

18. *Love Me Like You*
Midtempo sixties-inspired smoochathon to catch your breath and click your fingers to. 'Snap'.

19. *Weird People*
Like the perfect theme tune to a lost 80s comedy starring Bette Midler and Whoopi Goldberg. So cool, so funky, so weird.

20. *Secret Love Song*
Powerful emotion-packed climactic sing-a-long and the perfect tear-streaked finish to any good night.

"We wanna thank our fans, we would not be here without you mixers, we love you so much."
– *Leigh-Anne*

LITTLE MIX ♥
LITTLE MIXERS

"Mixers, where do we bloody start? We just love you so much, we do. There are no words to describe how incredible you guys are."
– Jesy

CREDITS